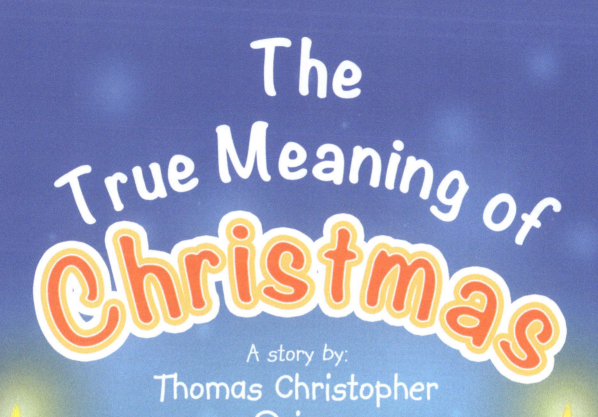

The True Meaning of Christmas

A story by:
Thomas Christopher Grimm

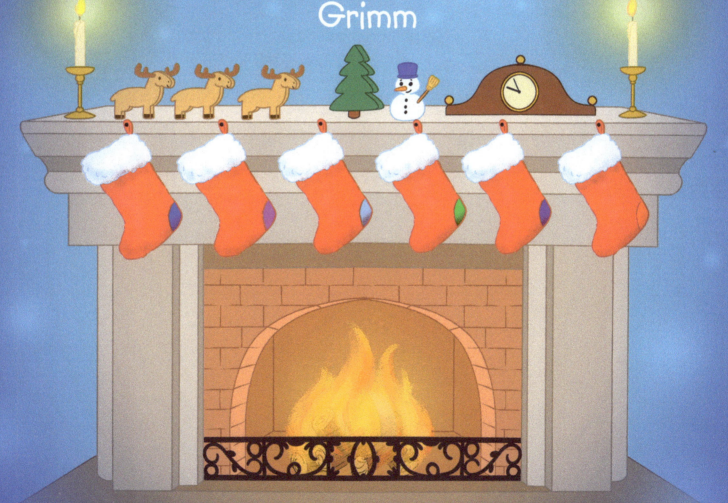

Illustrations by Mureson Radu

Copyright © 2024 Thomas Christopher Grimm.

All rights reserved. No part of this book may be used or reproduced by any means, graphic, electronic, or mechanical, including photocopying, recording, taping or by any information storage retrieval system without the written permission of the author except in the case of brief quotations embodied in critical articles and reviews.

Archway Publishing books may be ordered through booksellers or by contacting:

Archway Publishing
1663 Liberty Drive
Bloomington, IN 47403
www.archwaypublishing.com
844-669-3957

Because of the dynamic nature of the Internet, any web addresses or links contained in this book may have changed since publication and may no longer be valid. The views expressed in this work are solely those of the author and do not necessarily reflect the views of the publisher, and the publisher hereby disclaims any responsibility for them.

Interior Image Credit: Mureson Radu

IISBN: 978-1-6657-6501-5 (sc)
ISBN: 978-1-6657-6500-8 (hc)
ISBN: 978-1-6657-6499-5 (e)

Library of Congress Control Number: 2024917255

Print information available on the last page.

Archway Publishing rev. date: 10/10/2024

To my daughter and angel, Kasey;
her wonderful husband, Ryan;
and their four incredibly
amazing children,
(my grandchildren):
Maddie, Natalie, Harper, and Nolan.

It was hard to go to sleep just two days before Christmas because I was so excited for Santa Claus to come.

Tonight was worse because no sooner had I fallen asleep than I woke up hearing my little sister Harper in the next room coughing— *cough, cough, cough.*

How will I go back to sleep with the sound of Harper coughing? I asked myself. Yet I did fall asleep because I awoke again to the sound of Harper coughing.

Oh no, I thought. *Here we go again.* It was a long night, falling asleep and then waking up to the sounds of Harper coughing again and again and again.

Three times I heard my mom get up to check on Harper and help her sleep through her cough.

The next morning, I walked slowly downstairs for breakfast, feeling tired and hungry.

But then I got excited seeing that my mom had changed her Christmas sign to read, "One more sleep until Christmas."

My renewed excitement for Christmas made me forget about my hard night's sleep.

Cough, cough, cough. It was Harper coughing again.

This time the sound came from the couch in our playroom.

Only Harper wasn't playing. She was sitting on the couch with her bunny clutched to her chest as she coughed again.

Our sister, Natalie, who was seven and a year younger than me, sat next to Harper stroking her hair. Our baby brother, Nolan, lay nearby on a pillow on the floor finishing a bottle of milk.

"Shhh," whispered Natalie. "It will be OK."

"Oh dear, Harper," Mom said. "I'm going to have to call the doctor. I hope she doesn't say you need to go to the hospital again."

Mom said *again* because Harper had already gone to the hospital twice with a bad cough. But the last time was months ago. Mom and Dad were sure her breathing problems were over, but I guessed not.

Cough, cough! Harper barked a few more coughs.

"Hi, this is Kasey, Harper's mother," I heard my mom say on the phone. "My four-year old daughter, Harper, is not feeling well, coughing, and having trouble breathing. Can I speak with the nurse?"

After a pause to wait for the nurse to come on the phone, Mom said, "Hi, Ellen; Harper is having trouble breathing and coughing again. You will recall she had to go into the hospital a few months ago to get her oxygen levels up to a good level. What should I do?"

I could hear the nurse speaking to Mom, but I couldn't tell what she was saying. "OK," Mom said, "I'll take her to the hospital emergency room right away and I'll ask my husband, Ryan, to meet us there. Thank you; goodbye."

"OK, girls," Mom said to Natalie and me. "I'm going to need your help. The doctor wants me to take Harper to the emergency room. I'm going to call Tangkwa to come over and babysit Nolan and you girls, and I'm going to call Dad to meet us at the emergency room."

Oh no, I thought. *Here we go again*. But Natalie and I knew what to do. We ran upstairs and got a change of clothes for Harper and put them in a duffel bag for her, along with three of her books and her favorite bunny.

The doorbell rang, so we ran downstairs to open the door.

It was Tangkwa. We were so happy to see her.

"Tangkwa, Harper has to go to the hospital because she can't stop coughing," Natalie said.

"Oh no," Tangkwa replied. "Let's help Harper get ready."

We found Harper's shoes and coat for her. A few minutes later, we waved to Harper and Mom as they drove away.

Now what? I thought. *Christmas is just a day away, but Christmas won't be Christmas without Harper.*

Tangkwa interrupted my thoughts. "Come on, girls; let's clean up and eat lunch. I spoke to your dad. He is going to the hospital to meet your mom and Harper. And guess what? Your granddad is coming from Wilmington to help us get ready for Christmas."

"Hooray!" said Natalie. "Granddad always makes us laugh."

I was happy too, and I thought, *Maybe Granddad can help us feel like Christmas is still coming, even without Harper home with us.*

Before we knew it, Granddad had arrived with smiles and hugs for Natalie, Nolan, and me. But I was worried. I wondered inside whether Santa would still come if Harper wasn't home. And even if he did, would he leave presents for her?

"Granddad," I said, "is Santa still going to come even if Harper and Mom aren't home?"

"Absolutely," Granddad said. "Santa will not disappoint you because you have been so good all year long. But we have some things to do to get ready for Christmas. After all, today's Christmas Eve!

I talked to your mom on the phone. We need to go to the store and pick up a ham for Christmas dinner. We need to clear the area in front of the fireplace for Santa's landing spot when he comes, hang up your stockings on the mantle, and put out some snacks for Santa and his reindeer."

"Oh yes," I exclaimed, "and we need to wrap presents we got for Mom and Dad. Can you help us?"

"Absolutely," replied Granddad. "Let's get started with the presents first."

Natalie and I ran upstairs to find wrapping paper and bows.

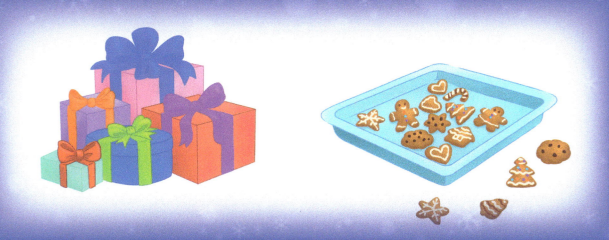

When we were finished wrapping the presents, Tangkwa took Nolan upstairs for his nap. Then Granddad and I jumped into his car to go pick up the ham, and Natalie and Tangkwa finished baking more Christmas cookies.

"I'm here to pick up a ham for my daughter, Kasey," Granddad told the clerk, a young woman with dark hair.

She looked at her computer, frowned, and said, "I'm sorry; I don't see an order for pickup today for Kasey.

"Oh, well, actually my daughter ordered the ham for pickup yesterday, but she was busy taking care of her sick daughter, so we are here today," replied Granddad.

"Do you have a receipt?" asked the clerk.

"No," Granddad replied.

"In that case, I need an email confirmation for your order. Do you have that?" the clerk asked.

"No." Granddad frowned. "I don't have that either, and my daughter Kasey is at the hospital. Let me try calling her." Granddad called Mom's cell phone, but she didn't answer.

I spoke up. "Granddad, maybe Mom can't talk on her phone at the hospital, but maybe she can text."

"Good idea," replied Granddad as he texted my mom.

After what seemed like an eternity, Granddad's phone chimed with a text from Mom, who sent us the confirmation we needed. Within minutes, we had our Christmas ham and were on our way.

Outside with Granddad, I said, "Wow, that was stressful, Granddad! Who knew it could be so hard to pick up a ham?"

"Sure was," Granddad said, sighing. "But you helped me find a solution. Let's make one more stop and pick up pizza for dinner tonight."

When we stopped for pizza, I asked Granddad to also buy some vanilla ice cream, Harper's favorite, in the hopes that Mom and Harper would come home in time for dinner.

When we got home, my heart leaped for joy because my dad's car was in the driveway, and I hoped that meant Harper was coming home. I ran into the house, yelling, "Daddy, is Harper coming home today?"

"No, pretty, she can't. The doctors say she must stay in the hospital tonight. In fact, after dinner, I need to go back to the hospital and take some pajamas for Harper and Mom to wear tonight. Let's hope Harper can come home tomorrow."

Natalie started to cry, which made me want to cry too.

"But it's Christmas Eve, Dad; the doctors have to let Harper come home," Natalie cried.

"Hey, girls," Granddad said, interrupting our tears, "let's eat our pizza and then get ready for Santa Claus and his reindeer. Tonight's the night!"

After dinner, Granddad said, "Natalie, you baked cookies with Tangkwa. Should we put some of them on a plate for Santa?"

"Sure," said Natalie. "The plate that Mom always uses for Santa's cookies is in there."

Natalie pointed to a cabinet above the microwave, and Granddad opened the cabinet and took down the plate.

Natalie and I piled it high with three different kinds of cookies.

Next, we went into the refrigerator to find carrots for Santa's reindeer.

"Let's put the carrots outside on the front porch," I exclaimed.

"Good idea," said Granddad. "Let's add some lettuce."

"The reindeer will enjoy a salad!" I said.

"Let's hang up our stockings on the fireplace mantle," said Natalie.

"Come with me, Natalie; I know where Mom stores our stockings—upstairs in a closet," I said.

Up the stairs we went and down the stairs we came with our stockings. Granddad had a hammer and hooks ready so we could hang our stockings on the mantle. *It's really looking a little bit more like Christmas now*, I thought.

Granddad clapped his hands and said, "It's time to get ready for bed, girls. Tangkwa has already put Nolan to bed. Your dad will be home from visiting Mom and Harper at the hospital soon. Let's surprise him and be all ready for bed."

"But we're too excited for bed," said Natalie. "Can't we play downstairs?"

"Not tonight, Natalie—after all, the sooner we all go to sleep, the sooner Santa will come," said Granddad.

"Can Natalie and I sleep together?" I asked.

"Sure," replied Granddad.

Natalie smiled, turned to me, and said, "Let's go, Maddie; I'll race you upstairs."

Natalie and I hurried to change into our pajamas, wash our hands and faces, and brush our teeth.

As we were climbing into bed, we heard the garage door opening. Daddy was home!

Dad came upstairs and smiled when he saw Natalie and me curled up together in my bed.

"Oh, you girls are sleeping together Christmas Eve? Great idea. Want me to read you some books?"

Daddy read us three books, kissed us on our foreheads, and said, "Sleep well, girls, and I'll see you on Christmas Day!"

The next morning, I felt a nudge. It was Natalie.

"Maddie," she whispered, "wake up; it's Christmas morning."

I bolted out of bed, and Natalie and I ran into Dad's bedroom to wake him up.

"Merry Christmas, Daddy!" we screamed.

"Merry Christmas, girls," Dad replied. "Let's go downstairs and see what Santa brought!"

Dad went down the stairs first, and we followed holding hands as we hurried downstairs. Granddad was downstairs with Nolan already and waiting for us with his camera.

"Merry Christmas, girls!" exclaimed Granddad.

"Merry Christmas, Granddad," we sang. Natalie and I held Nolan's hands as Granddad took our picture in front of our fireplace.

But my smile was fading at the thought of celebrating Christmas without Mom and Harper.

Dad pointed to the Christmas plate by the fireplace that we had piled high with cookies last night.

"Oh my gosh," I said. "Look, guys, all the cookies are gone except one. I guess Santa was hungry."

We scurried to our stockings and quickly took them down from the mantle. Dad slowed us down, saying, "Girls, since Harper isn't here, how about we open our stockings and just one present each and wait for Mom and Harper before opening the other presents?"

"Daddy, please, please, can we open all our presents?" I begged.

"No," Dad replied. "I think we should wait."

"Oh jeez, OK," said Natalie.

Natalie and I pulled out many different small surprises from our stockings, screaming when we found bubble bath, Life Savers, and lip gloss.

We then each chose one present under the tree to open. Natalie opened a small toy dollhouse, smiled, and handed it to Dad, asking "Can you help me put this together, Daddy?"

I tore open the paper on my present and was excited to see it was a drawing board with colored pencils.

Natalie and I looked at the other presents under the tree, and together we asked, "Daddy, can we open a few more presents please?"

"Not now, girls—remember I said one present for each of you."

I was not happy to hear that. PLEASE, Dad!" I pleaded. I was beginning to feel a bit sorry for myself.

"Hey, girls," Granddad said, interrupting, "I wonder whether the reindeer liked the lettuce and carrots."

We raced to the front door and out onto the porch. "Look!" exclaimed Natalie. "Some of the carrots are gone, and those two carrots look like the reindeer gnawed on them. And the lettuce is all gone."

"They were super hungry, I guess," I replied.

Natalie and I went inside, and the sad feeling came back to me when I looked at all the unopened presents under the tree.

This is not a good Christmas at all, I thought.

"What can we do now, Dad?" Natalie asked.

"Let's put your new dollhouse together," he replied.

"What about me?" I asked.

"How about you and I find a game to play?" said Granddad.

"I don't really feel like playing a game," I said. "I just want to open more presents." I thought opening more presents would make my sad feeling go away.

"Well, you know we decided to wait for Mom and Harper before we open more presents right now," Granddad reminded me.

I felt a pang of sadness in my tummy again, and I frowned. I felt like I was going to cry.

But then I heard the garage door opening. *Could it be?* I thought. "Maybe Mommy and Harper are home," I exclaimed. "Come on, Natalie; let's see."

Natalie and I ran to the front door and looked out to the driveway.

Sure enough, it was Mommy and Harper. We opened the front door and ran to Mom's car screaming, "Harper, Harper!" We could see Harper in the backseat. She had a huge smile on her face.

Mommy hugged Natalie and me, saying, "It looks like you girls missed us."

"We sure did; it wasn't Christmas without you," Natalie and I shouted.

"Come on, Harper," said Natalie. "We have lots of presents to open with you." Harper followed Natalie into the house as fast as their legs could carry them.

As I happily watched Natalie and Harper tear into their presents, the presents under the tree didn't seem so important to me anymore. "Santa brought me the doll baby I wanted," squealed Harper.

"Oh my gosh," shouted Natalie, "more Legos for me to build!" Even baby Nolan let out a screech.

Looking around and seeing the smiles on my parents' faces, I realized the knot in my stomach was gone. My sadness had been replaced by a warm feeling inside.

Christmas really seemed like Christmas now.

Mom said, "Maddie, you aren't opening any of your presents, but you look so happy."

"I'm just so happy my whole family is home together for Christmas," I said, sighing. "It's all I could ever want."

Mom smiled too and said, "Maybe this year you girls learned the true meaning of Christmas."

Printed in the USA
CPSIA information can be obtained
at www.ICGtesting.com
CBHW041506221024
16243CB00011B/130